Lisa Prange · Rebecca Sprengel

This and That

*Aktivitäten
für den Englischunterricht*

Max Hueber Verlag

Das Werk und seine Teile sind urheberrechtlich geschützt.
Jede Verwertung in anderen als den gesetzlich zugelassenen
Fällen bedarf deshalb der vorherigen schriftlichen
Einwilligung des Verlages.

3. 2. 1. | Die letzten Ziffern
2000 1999 98 97 96 | bezeichnen Zahl und Jahr des Druckes.
Alle Drucke dieser Auflage können, da unverändert,
nebeneinander benutzt werden.
1. Auflage
© 1996 Max Hueber Verlag, D-85737 Ismaning
Verlagsredaktion: Cornelia Dietz
Umschlaggestaltung: Zembsch' Werkstatt, München
Layout: Erentraut Waldau, Ismaning
Zeichnungen: Heinrich Haisch, München
Satz: Design-Typo-Print GmbH, Ismaning
Druck: Ludwig Auer, Donauwörth
Printed in Germany
ISBN 3–19–002435–9

Contents

Preface	4
Card games	5
1 Indiscreet questions	6
2 Snap	8
3 Swapping game	11
4 What is it?	13
Agreeing and disagreeing games	17
5 Likes and dislikes	18
6 Things we have done	19
7 Childhood memories	20
8 Feelings	21
9 This and that	22
10 Preposition merry-go-round	23
Information gap games	25
11 People in our street 1	26
12 People in our street 2	28
13 Family photo	30
Negotiating games	33
14 My diary	34
15 How well do you know each other?	36
16 Doodles	38
17 Morning routine	40
18 What's the reason?	42
19 Optimist and pessimist	44
20 Let's spend Saturday together	46
Board games	49
Snakes and ladders	49
21 In a restaurant	50
22 Could I …?	52
23 Spot the preposition	54
24 Fill the gaps	56
Dice and board games	59
25 Dreams and wishes	60
26 Who says what?	62
27 How often? – When? – How long?	64
28 What do you prefer?	66
29 Comparing	68
30 Opinion survey	70
31 Where would I use it?	72
32 The clock	74
33 Comparatives and superlatives	76
34 Vocabulary board	78
Dialogue games	81
35 Let's go to London	82
36 Meeting a friend	83
37 Your neighbour's groceries	84
38 Which present?	86
39 Where can I go?	88
40 Can you help me?	90
41 Excuse me, but …	92
42 Don't worry …	94
43 Make a suggestion	96
44 In the bookstore	98
Key to the information gap games 11, 12 and 13	99
Index	100

Preface

This and That is a collection of 44 communicative games for learners of English of all ages and levels. They can be used in most teaching situations. The teacher can fit them in to the teaching programme at any stage, either to consolidate what has just been taught, as a revision, to recycle and reactivate language or as a communicative activity standing on its own. I have also found these games very useful during intensive courses, even ESP courses, to liven up the group when energy levels are low.

I have kept the *rules and instructions* as simple as possible so that the teacher can adapt the games to his own style and situation. Very little preparation is needed. All you need to do is make the copies – which can be re-used – and bring along for example dice and/or matches. The games can be used with groups of any size (min. 2 students).

The levels indicated are only to be seen as guidelines, as most games are elastic and can be adapted to the individual class situation. As an example: by putting in appropriate sentences on the boards of the *Snakes and ladders* activities, the teacher can use the games at post-beginner or advanced level.

The *time* (duration) is an approximate minimum, which includes setting up and explaining the game. If the students are involved and producing a lot of language, it is advisable to let them take all the time they want.

A few general thoughts:
– Different groups have 'favourite' games and enjoy playing them several times.
– The student generated teacher can even encourage the students to create their own games based on the activities in this book or on the games they know.
– The dice-throwing and arguing energises and enlivens the group atmosphere in a way that most students do not associate with language learning.
– Everybody is working at the same time, which means a period of intense involvement.

Finally, although the majority of English teachers are female, I have used the masculine form for reasons of brevity and style.

Rebecca Sprengel
Lisa Prange

Card games

It is advisable to glue the copies onto thin cardboard before cutting out the cards.

Card games

1 Indiscreet questions

3-6 Players

Cards

Level 2

45 min.

Players form a circle. Shuffle the cards and lay them face down on the table.

The first player picks up a card and asks the person on his right the question on the card. He must answer the question honestly even if the question is indiscreet. He must also state a reason if the card requires it.

The player who has just answered picks up a card and asks the player on his right.

When all the cards have been used, reshuffle them and start again. If a player gets asked the same question, he may put this question to someone else.

Card games

What was the happiest time of your life?	Where would you like to live?	Name a terrible person.	What are you afraid of?	In which situation have you told a lie?	Who has had a great influence in your life?	What is your favourite dish?	Describe your best friend.
Which is your favourite country? Why?	Who would you like to spend time with?	What do you do in your spare time?	What would you like to change about yourself? Why?	What are your plans for the future?	Do you like parties? Why/Why not?	Which professions do you find interesting? Why?	What do you get angry about the most?
Which book have you enjoyed reading?	What do you like to remember?	Which animal would you like to be? Why?	What would you do if you won a milion pounds?	What makes you happy?	Which famous person would you like to spend a day with?	Do you play an instrument? If not, which one would you like to play?	Name something you regret not having done.

7

Card games

3-6 Players

2 Snap   Zugreifen

Cards

The cards should be well shuffled. Give out an equal number of cards to all players. Each player should have roughly the same amount of *sentence cards* and *tag cards.*

The first player reads out a sentence. The others look at their cards to find a tag that fits. The player who thinks he has got the fitting tag should shout *snap* as quickly as possible. He then reads out the tag.

Level 1

If the answer is right, both players lay their cards aside and the player who had the tag reads out another sentence. If he was wrong, the first player reads out his sentence again until the right tag is found.

The winner is the first person to get rid of all his cards.
   loswein

30 min.

You are married	He's German	You don't like him	He lost the game
She didn't write	You're not French	He's late	They didn't go home
I'm wonderful	You've been here before	She's right	They work very hard
He's an actor	I'm not very old	She went to London	He didn't phone his mother
You've been to the hairdresser's	He hasn't done his homework	I gave you the money	You studied French

Card games

didn't he?	do you?	isn't he?	aren't you?
did they?	isn't he?	are you?	did she?
don't they?	isn't she?	haven't you?	aren't I?
did he?	didn't she?	am I?	isn't he?
didn't you?	didn't I?	has he?	haven't you?

Card games

3 Swapping game

3-6 Players

Cards

Paper and pencil

Level 3

Each player should write three of his most important qualities on a piece of paper.

Players then form a circle and are given an equal number of cards (minimum three, maximum six). Remove remaining cards from the game.

The objective of the game is for each player to try and get the qualities he is missing and would like to have by swapping. As the player doesn't know what is on the other cards, he must start by asking the others which qualities they would like to have.

The first player asks player 2 for a quality he would like to have himself. If player 2 has the card with the quality on it, he must give it to player 1. Player 2 gets another card in return from player 1. If player 2 does not have the card then player 1 can ask another player. He should be able to do this a limited number of times depending on the number of players. Player 1 can ask for the desired card directly or lay one of the cards he doesn't want on the table face up and offer to swap it. Once player 1 has either got the card he was looking for, or has run out of questions, then it is the next player's turn.

As the game goes on, the players will realize what is on the cards and who has them. They will then be able to ask more direct questions.

> I have sense of humour.
> I don't need it. I already have a sense of humour.
> You are so patient already. Give me your patience.
> Are you clever?
> Would you swap your intelligence for my success?

30 min.

Card games

Beauty	Helpfulness	Musicality
Stamina	Strength	Artistic nature
Success	Calm	Good taste
Patience	Tolerance	Good at languages
Punctuality	Courage	Imagination
Intelligence	Energy	Friendliness
Cleverness	Confidence	Wit
Sense of humour	Optimism	Good with your hands

4 What is it?   *Schummellieschen*

3-6 Players

Cards

Level 3

30 min.

Every player is dealt five cards. Place the remaining cards face down in a pile on the table. Turn the first card over.

The first player tries to think of an object that fits the description on the card on the table and on one of his cards. He then lays that card, face up, on top of the first card without naming the object he is thinking of. The next player does the same and so on.
If a player hasn't got a card, he has to pick one from the pile, and, if it fits the others he can then put it on the other cards.

A player can try and trick the others by putting a card down even though he hasn't been able to think of an object. By doing this, he is taking a risk: if another player notices, he can ask him to name the object. If he can't, he has to pick up all the cards except the first card that had been turned over at the start of the game.

The player who asked the question is also taking a risk, as, if the player he asked does have the answer, then the player who asked the question will have to pick up all the cards.

If all the cards have been used, turn the pile over, shuffle and start again. The pack has two *jokers* that can be used instead of a card if a player hasn't got the right card.

The first to be left without any cards is the winner.

Card games

Can be held in one's hand	Used in the office	Is drunk warm or cold	Must be washed after use	Made of wood	Can be hung on the wall	Sometimes taken on trips	One can hide behind it
Some people get angry about it	Used mainly by women	Is imported from Africa	Is thrown away after use	Is peeled and then eaten	Is produced in factories	Didn't exist 100 years ago	One can wear it
Normally used by men	Can be eaten warm or cold	Is often borrowed	Is turned on before use	Mainly men are interested in it	Joker	Costs a lot of money	Used at work

Card games

Is found in a department store	One can eat it	
Breaks easily	Costs less than 20 pounds	
		One shouldn't lend it
A lot of people enjoy it	One can put something in it	Every home has one
One can sit on it	*Joker*	Shouldn't be seen on your desk at work
Mainly women are interested in it	Children love it	Often given as a present
One often owns several	Good for one's health	I would never leave the house without it
Most people would like to own one	Not very useful	Made of plastic
Used in the home	Difficult to operate	Very useful
	Made of leather	

15

Agreeing and disagreeing games

These games are cooperative games for small groups of 2 or 3 players.

Rules:

All players should agree on how to complete the sentence.
Each player suggests a solution and asks the others if they agree. If a player does not agree he should give his reason and, if possible, offer an alternative. The players should discuss the alternatives until an agreement is reached.

Agreeing and disagreeing games

2-3 Players

Level 1

20 min.

5 Likes and dislikes

▶ See page 17 for rules

> I like books a lot. Do you? – Yes, I do.
> No, I don't, because …
>
> What do you think of this book? – I think it's good.
> I don't think it is good, because …
>
> Do you like to drink mineral water? – Yes, I do.
> No, I don't, I prefer to drink wine.

a) We like _____ .

b) We don't like _____ .

c) We like to play _____ .

d) We think _____ is very interesting.

e) We hate _____ .

f) We think _____ is terrible.

g) We don't like to drink _____ .

h) We love _____ .

i) We like to eat _____ .

j) We think _____ is funny.

k) We like to _____ .

l) We like to drink _____ .

Agreeing and disagreeing games

6 Things we have done

▶ See page 17 for rules

2-3 Players

Level 1

20 min.

| I have | often / sometimes | eaten pizza. – I have too. / Me too. |
| | | I haven't. |

I have never been to Italy. – I haven't either.
                                But I have.
Have you ever eaten pizza? – Yes, I have.
                            No, I haven't.
Have you ever been to Italy? – Yes, I have.
                               No, I haven't.
Have you ever lost your keys? – Yes, I have.
                                No, I haven't.

a) We have never been to _____ .

b) We have never drunk _____ .

c) We have both/all once lost _____ .

d) We have both/all read _____ .

e) We have both/all often forgotten _____ .

f) We have both/all been to _____ .

g) We have never eaten _____ .

h) We have both/all bought _____ .

i) We have both/all drunk _____ .

j) We have both/all eaten _____ .

k) We have never seen _____ .

Agreeing and disagreeing games

7 Childhood memories

2-3 Players

Level 2

20 min.

▶ See page 17 for rules

When I was little, I always wanted to stay up late.
        I was never allowed to stay up late.

When I was young, I always had to look after my little brother.

I was never very good | at maths at school.
I was quite good

As a child, I used to hate spinach.
        I used to love chocolate.

How about you? – Yes, I/we did/had too.
        No, I/we didn't/hadn't.
        So was I. / So were we.
        Neither was I. / Neither were we.
        So could/had I/we.
        Neither could/had I/we.

a) When we were young, we always wanted to _____ .

b) As children, we were not allowed to _____ .

c) At home we always had to _____ .

d) We were afraid of _____ as children.

e) We _____ for the first time when we were ____ years old.

f) When we were eight, we _____ .

g) We used to be very interested in _____ as children.

h) When we were small, we used to like _____ .

i) We couldn't yet _____ when we were seven.

j) We used to hate _____ .

k) We learnt to _____ when we were ____ years old.

l) We both/all had _____ when we were children.

m) We used to _____ with our friends.

n) We used to _____ when we were alone.

o) At school, we _____ .

p) We didn't use to have _____ as children.

Agreeing and disagreeing games

8 Feelings

▶ See page 17 for rules

2-3 Players

Level 2

20 min.

| I | often / usually / sometimes | feel | happy / angry | when/if | ... |

| I am | disappointed about/with / satisfied with / proud of | ... |

I am afraid of ...

| I get | angry / sad | when/if | ... |

How about you? Do you feel the same way? – Yes, I do.
　　　　　　　　　　　　　　　　　　　　　No, I don't.

a) We feel happy when/if _____ .

b) We get angry _____ .

c) We feel disappointed when/if _____ .

d) We are satisfied _____ .

e) We worry _____ .

f) We are afraid _____ .

g) We are proud of _____ .

h) We feel embarrassed when/if _____ .

i) We feel stressed _____ .

j) We feel bored when/if _____ .

k) We get insecure when/if _____ .

l) We feel amused when/if _____ .

m) We feel silly when/if _____ .

Agreeing and disagreeing games

9 This and that

2-3 Players

Level 3

20 min.

▶ See page 17 for rules

I think	that ...
I feel	
My opinion is	

What do you think/feel? — Yes, I think so too.
What's your opinion?   Yes, I agree.
                         Well, I see your point, but ...
                         I'm afraid I can't agree with you on that.
                         No, I don't think so, on the contrary ...

a) We think good friends _____ .

b) We really think that politicians _____ .

c) In our opinion, it is wrong _____ .

d) We think a good teacher _____ .

e) We think that life a hundred years ago _____ .

f) We think it's right that/for _____ .

g) We like people who _____ .

h) We hope _____ .

i) We think that all people _____ .

j) We think that human beings shouldn't _____ .

k) Love means _____ to us.

l) In our opinion, today's youth _____ .

m) Our opinion is that _____ is very disturbing.

n) In our opinion, one should _____ .

22

10 Preposition merry-go-round

2-3 Players

Level 2

▶ See page 17 for rules.

Variation
Pairs or groups of three should complete the sentences together quietly within a time limit. Students then pair up or regroup with others to compare and, if necessary, improve results. By helping each other, the class will, hopefully, come up with all the right answers in the end.

20 min.

Use the right preposition:

a) He's interested _____ old cars.

b) This is my first visit _____ Norway.

c) I go to work _____ bus.

d) I'll meet you _____ Monday.

e) Come _____ a drink tomorrow.

f) He is always talking _____ his work.

g) She works _____ an international firm.

h) Look _____ that girl, isn't she beautiful?

i) She grew up _____ York.

j) I saw him _____ the dentist's.

k) Agatha was born _____ 1928.

l) When having a meal, people usually sit _____ the table.

m) Granny drove _____ a tree yesterday.

n) That music has a strange effect _____ me.

o) You will have to explain it _____ them again.

p) She was shaking _____ anger.

q) I've just read a novel _____ Jane Austen.

r) What are you doing _____ the weekend?

s) What a clever boy! He made it all _____ himself.

t) Now we are all good _____ using the right prepositions.

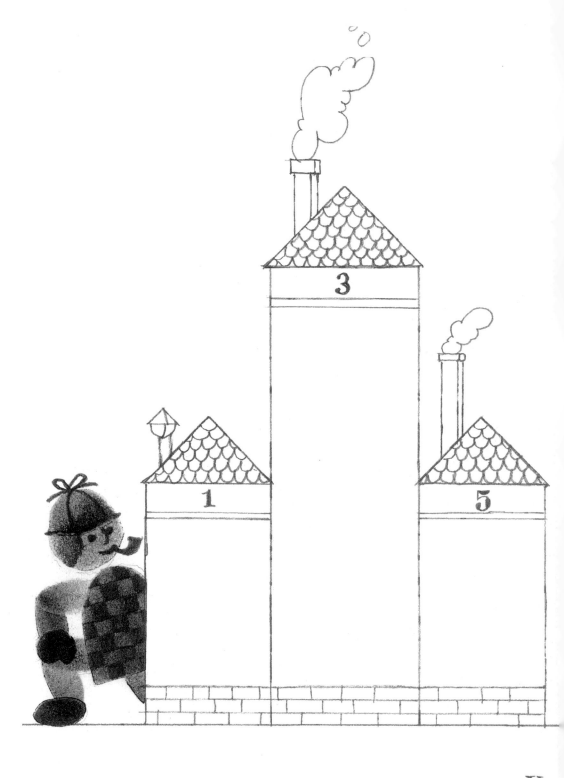

q   H
     J
Q.   m   k

Information gap games

These are games for 2 players.

Each player only has half the information but has to fill in the same diagram. The two players can do this by asking each other questions and providing information.

Answers on page 99

Information gap games

11 People in our street 1

2 Players

Pen and paper

Level 2

20 min.

Player A

There are five houses and one person in each house. Find out as much as you can about these five people by sharing information with your partner. Fill the information into the diagram.

	No. 1	No. 3	No. 5	No. 7	No. 9
Name					
Age					
Profession					
Hobbies					
Food/drink					

Your information:

a) The woman who likes swimming and the child are neighbours.

b) The old man does not work. He's an old age pensioner.

c) One of the women likes coffee. She has no time for hobbies.

d) The OAP and the salesman have the same hobby.

e) Steven's neighbour is only seven years old and she goes to school.

f) Steven is seventeen.

g) The woman police officer likes wine.

h) Mr Winterbottom lives in No. 9.

i) Emma likes to ride her bike.

j) Joan French is 39.

Information gap games

11 People in our street 1

Player B

There are five houses and one person in each house. Find out as much as you can about these five people by sharing information with your partner. Fill the information into the diagram.

	No. 1	No. 3	No. 5	No. 7	No. 9
Name					
Age					
Profession					
Hobbies					
Food/drink					

Your information:

a) One of the people likes meat and reads a lot.
b) Both the OAP and the child like spaghetti.
c) Mr Winterbottom is 89 years old and his neighbour is 57.
d) Steven lives between Emma and Fiona Waters.
e) The woman from No.1 often goes swimming.
f) Emma is only seven.
g) The woman who lives in No.7 has no hobbies.
h) The boy works as a salesman.
i) Mrs Waters is a doctor.
j) One of the women is a police officer.

Information gap games

2 Players

12 People in our street 2

Player A

Pen and paper

There are 5 houses and one person in each house. Find out as much as you can about these people by sharing the information with your neighbour. Fill the information into the diagram.

Level 2

20 min.

	No. 1	No. 3	No. 5	No. 7	No. 9
Name					
Marital status					
No. of children					
Profession					
Hobbies					

Your information:

a) Fred Taylor is a widower. His neighbour is a divorced woman.

b) The woman who lives in No.1 has two daughters.

c) There are no children in No.7.

d) The woman who has one daughter likes reading.

e) Julia Richards is a hairdresser.

f) The woman who is married likes to play tennis.

g) The widower and the single woman both like reading.

h) The single man is a bank manager.

i) Audrey Parker has one daughter.

j) There are a total of six children in all five houses: three boys and three girls.

12 People in our street 2

Player B

There are 5 houses and one person in each house. Find out as much as you can about these people by sharing the information with your neighbour. Fill the information into the diagram.

	No. 1	No. 3	No. 5	No. 7	No. 9
Name					
Marital status					
No. of children					
Profession					
Hobbies					

Your information:

a) The married woman is a housewife.

b) One little girl lives in No. 3.

c) Fred Taylor lives in No. 9.

d) Andrew Wright lives between Audrey and Julia.

e) The man who likes to swim lives with his son.

f) Fred doesn't work, he's an old age pensioner.

g) The woman who lives next to the single man has a daughter and is a teacher.

h) Jean is married.

i) The woman who likes photography has no children.

j) The single woman with a daughter does not live next to the man with two sons.

Information gap games

2 Players

Pen and paper

Level 2

20 min.

13 Family photo

Player A

There are six people standing next to each other on the family photo. What do you know about these people? Work with your neighbour (player B) and write the information onto the sheet below.

Name						
Relation-ship to others						
Hobbies						
Age						

Your information:

a) Michael's great-aunt likes needlework.

b) Steven's mother likes to paint and so does her grandson.

c) There is a 34 year old man on the far right of the photo.

d) Michael is standing on his grandmother's left.

e) Sophie's niece is called Joanne.

f) Sophie's father-in-law is called Paul.

g) Steven is standing on the right of his grandfather. Steven's grandfather likes to read.

h) Steven's aunt is called Charlotte and is 58 years old.

i) Paul's grandson is Sophie's son.

j) The women on the photo are 58, 62 and 29 years old.

13 Family photo

Player B

There are six people standing next to each other on a family photo. What do you know about these people? Work with your neighbour (player A) and write the information onto the sheet below.

Name						
Relation-ship to others						
Hobbies						
Age						

Your information:

a) Paul's great-grandson is five years old.
b) The thirty-four year old man is called Steven.
c) Steven's girl cousin likes walking.
d) Paul's great-grandson's name is Michael.
e) Charlotte's daughter is standing between her and Michael.
f) Sophie's sister is standing on the far left.
g) Charlotte's nephew likes to play tennis.
h) Paul's daughter-in-law is standing between him and his great-grandson.
i) Paul's grandson is 34 years old.
j) The oldest man on the photo is 86 years old.

Negotiating games

Negotiating games are cooperative games for two players (three players required for game No. 20: *Let's spend Saturday together*).

Negotiating games

2 Players

Pen and paper

Level 1

30 min.

14 My diary

Player A

You want or have to do the following this week:

go to the doctor
attend a one-day conference in another town
entertain foreign visitors
go to the cinema
go to a yoga class
have a three hour meeting with your boss
spend four hours at the gym
clean the house
go to the supermarket

1. Write your plans into your diary. By the way, you like going to bed early.

2. You would like to learn English with B. Look at your calendar and make an appointment with him.

> Are you free at … o'clock? – Yes, that would be fine. I don't have anything planned.
> Yes, I could make that.
>
> Could we meet on … | morning? | – No, I'm afraid that won't be possible.
> | afternoon? | I need to … .
> | evening? | I would like to … .

3. When you have made your appointment, write it into your diary. Think of other things you could do together and ask him. Then write these into your diary too.

> Would you like to … with me? – Yes, I would. When should we …
> No, not really, but how about …

13 Monday	**14** Tuesday	**15** Wednesday	**16** Thursday	**17** Friday	**18** Saturday	**19** Sunday
7	7	7	7	7	7	7
8	8	8	8	8	8	8
9	9	9	9	9	9	9
10	10	10	10	10	10	10
11	11	11	11	11	11	11
12	12	12	12	12	12	12
13	13	13	13	13	13	13
14	14	14	14	14	14	14
15	15	15	15	15	15	15
16	16	16	16	16	16	16
17	17	17	17	17	17	17
18	18	18	18	18	18	18
19	19	19	19	19	19	19
20	20	20	20	20	20	20
21	21	21	21	21	21	21
22	22	22	22	22	22	22

14 My diary

Player B

You want or have to do the following:

1. Write your plans into your diary. By the way, you like sleeping late in the morning.

2. You would like to learn English with A. Look at your calendar and make an appointment with him.

> Are you free at ... o'clock? – Yes, that would be fine. I don't have anything planned.
> Yes, I could make that.
>
> Could we meet on ... | morning? | – No, I'm afraid that won't be possible.
> | afternoon? | I need to ... .
> | evening? | I would like to ... .

3. When you have made your appointment, write it into your diary. Think of other things you could do together and ask him. Then write these into your diary too.

> Would you like to ... with me? – Yes, I would. When should we ...
> No, not really, but how about ...

13 Monday	14 Tuesday	15 Wednesday	16 Thursday	17 Friday	18 Saturday	19 Sunday
7	7	7	7	7	7	7
8	8	8	8	8	8	8
9	9	9	9	9	9	9
10	10	10	10	10	10	10
11	11	11	11	11	11	11
12	12	12	12	12	12	12
13	13	13	13	13	13	13
14	14	14	14	14	14	14
15	15	15	15	15	15	15
16	16	16	16	16	16	16
17	17	17	17	17	17	17
18	18	18	18	18	18	18
19	19	19	19	19	19	19
20	20	20	20	20	20	20
21	21	21	21	21	21	21
22	22	22	22	22	22	22

Negotiating games

15 How well do you know each other?

2 Players

Pen and paper

Level 2

30 min.

Player A

1. Complete the following sentences in writing and say what is true for you. Then complete the sentences a second time with what you think is true about B.

Example:
When I am bored I go to the cinema.
I think that when you are bored you phone someone.

a) When I am bored I _____ .

b) When I am alone I _____ .

c) When I'm stressed _____ .

d) When the alarm clock goes off in the morning I _____ .

e) When people visit me unannounced _____ .

f) If others laugh at me _____ .

g) If I find a fifty pound note _____ .

h) I feel happy if _____ .

i) I feel angry when _____ .

j) I feel content when _____ .

k) I feel proud if _____ .

l) I feel embarrassed if _____ .

m) I worry if _____ .

n) I need to laugh when _____ .

2. Now tell B what you think is true for him. He will tell you if you are right.

3. B will now tell you what he thinks is true for you. Tell him whether he is right or not and correct him if neccessary.

Yes, that's right/true.
No, that's not quite right/true.
No, I'm afraid that's (completely) wrong.

36

15 How well do you know each other?

Player B

1. *Complete the following sentences in writing and say what is true for you. Then complete the sentences a second time with what you think is true about A.*

> *Example:*
> When I am bored I go to the cinema.
> I think that when you are bored you phone someone.

a) When I am bored I _____ .

b) When I am alone I _____ .

c) When I'm stressed _____ .

d) When the alarm clock goes off in the morning I _____ .

e) When people visit me unannounced _____ .

f) If others laugh at me _____ .

g) If I find a fifty pound note _____ .

h) I feel happy if _____ .

i) I feel angry when _____ .

j) I feel content when _____ .

k) I feel proud if _____ .

l) I feel embarrassed if _____ .

m) I worry if _____ .

n) I need to laugh when _____ .

2. *A will now tell you what he thinks is true for you. Tell him whether he is right or not and correct him if neccessary.*

> Yes, that's right/true.
> No, that's not quite right/true.
> No, I'm afraid that's (completely) wrong.

3. *Now tell A what you think is true for him. He will tell you if you are right.*

Negotiating games

2 Players

Level 2

20 min.

16 Doodles

Player A

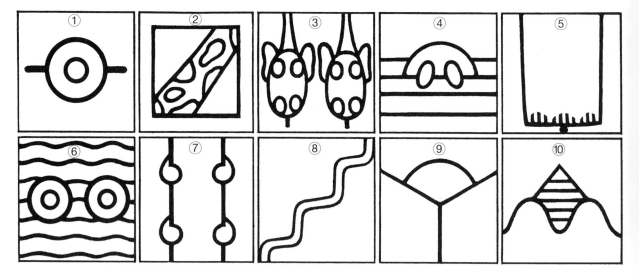

1. With your partner, try and guess what these "doodles" could be. You have a few hints, B has other hints.

> Example:
> Number 1 could be a Mexican (A) riding a bicycle (B).

two elephants	walking past a pyramid
a woman	scratching an ant's back
a Mexican	walking past a window
a man	swimming in the sea
a bear	creeping up the steps

2. Are there other solutions? Try and find as many as you can with B.

Couldn't Number 6 also be some glasses swimming in water?

I think Number 5 is a piece of wood on a pea.

Number 8 could be the tracks of a skier doing slalom.

16 Doodles

Player B

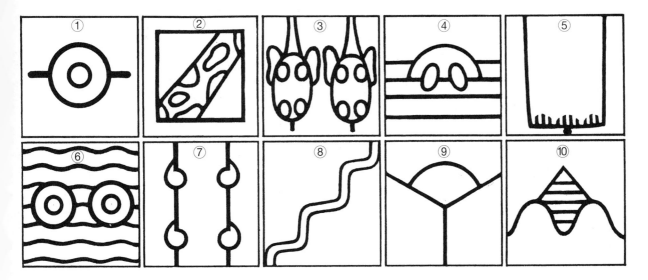

1. With your partner, try and guess what these "doodles" could be. You have a few hints, A has other hints.

> Example:
> Number 1 could be a Mexican (A) riding a bicycle (B).

a snake	cleaning the stairs
two Mexicans	climbing a tree
an elephant	reading the paper
a camel	sunbathing
a giraffe	riding a bicycle

2. Are there other solutions? Try and find as many as you can with A.

Couldn't Number 6 also be some glasses swimming in water?

I think Number 5 is a piece of wood on a pea.

Number 8 could be the tracks of a skier doing slalom.

Negotiating games

2 Players

Pen and paper

Level 1

30 min.

17 Morning routine

Player A

In which sequence do people do things? What do they do at the same time? Number the different activities.

Example:

	②	①	③
John:	clean his teeth –	have breakfast –	listen to the news
or:	②	①	①
	clean his teeth –	have breakfast –	listen to the news

Barbara: ○ get dressed – ○ put her make-up on – ○ have coffee

Charles: ○ shave – ○ listen to the weather forecast – ○ read the paper

Doris: ○ iron her blouse – ○ have breakfast – ○ get the milk in

Ian: ○ pack his satchel – ○ get washed – ○ comb his hair

Eddie: ○ smoke a cigarette – ○ have a cup of tea – ○ go to the bathroom

Fiona: ○ put in her contact lenses – ○ sing – ○ have a bath

1. Tell B what you think and he will tell you whether you have made the right guesses.

2. B has to guess about other people. Look at the information below and tell him where he was right.

George: ② make sandwiches for work – ① look for his glasses – ③ eat an egg

Helen: ③ have a shower – ① wake her husband – ② make coffee

James: ① get up – ② look in the mirror – ③ put the kettle on

Sarah: ③ dry her hair – ② have a shower – ① have breakfast

Jane: ① eat a slice of toast – ① listen to the news – ② look for her keys

Kevin: ② look out of the window – ③ get dressed – ① clean his teeth

17 Morning routine

Player B

In which sequence do people do things? What do they do at the same time? Number the different activities.

Example:

John: ② clean his teeth – ① have breakfast – ③ listen to the news
or: ② clean his teeth – ① have breakfast – ① listen to the news

George: ○ make sandwiches for work – ○ look for his glasses – ○ eat an egg
Helen: ○ have a shower – ○ wake her husband – ○ make coffee
James: ○ get up – ○ look in the mirror – ○ put the kettle on
Sarah: ○ dry her hair – ○ have a shower – ○ have breakfast
Jane: ○ eat a slice of toast – ○ listen to the news – ○ look for her keys
Kevin: ○ look out of the window – ○ get dressed – ○ clean his teeth

1. *A has to guess about other people. Look at the information below and tell him where he was right.*

Barbara: ② get dressed – ③ put her make-up on – ① have coffee
Charles: ① shave – ① listen to the weather forecast – ② read the paper
Doris: ① iron her blouse – ③ have breakfast – ② get the milk in
Ian: ③ pack his satchel – ② get washed – ① comb his hair
Eddie: ② smoke a cigarette – ① have a cup of tea – ③ go to the bathroom
Fiona: ② put in her contact lenses – ① sing – ① have a bath

2. *Tell A what you think and he will tell you whether you have made the right guesses.*

Negotiating games

18 What's the reason?

2 Players

Level 2

30 min.

Player A

1. *Read the following sentences and try to guess the reasons. You have 5 tries per sentence. Tell B what you think and he will tell you whether you are right.*

> *Example:*
> Kevin is going home earlier today.
> Why is Kevin going home earlier today? – Maybe he is expecting visitors.

a) Mary is a bit nervous this morning.

b) Penny is on the phone for 8 hours every day.

c) Anthony doesn't want to get married.

d) Bob stands in front of the mirror for hours every day.

e) Helen speaks very good German.

f) Frank has a headache this morning.

2. *B will now try to guess the reasons for his sentences. You have the correct information below, so tell B if his guess is right. He has 5 tries per sentence.*

a) Oliver never watches videos because he has no video recorder.

b) Sam is very tired today because he was up all night reading.

c) Sue needs change because she wants to buy cigarettes from the vending machine.

d) Mrs Tyler has not spoken to her husband for two days because he is on a business trip.

e) Many people do not like going to Mary Jenkins because she's a dentist.

f) Gary is in hospital visiting his sister.

42

18 What's the reason?

Player B

1. *A will try and guess the reasons for his sentences. You have the correct information below, so tell A if his guess is right. He has 5 tries per sentence.*

a) Mary is a bit nervous this morning because she has a dentist's appointment this afternoon.

b) Penny is on the phone eight hours a day because she works for directory enquiries.

c) Anthony doesn't want to get married because he is already married.

d) Bob stands in front of the mirror all day because he is a hairdresser.

e) Helen speaks very good German because she studied in Germany.

f) Frank has a headache this morning because he drank too much last night.

2. *Read the following sentences and try to guess the reasons. You have 5 tries per sentence. Tell A what you think and he will tell you whether you are right.*

> *Example:*
> Kevin is going home earlier today.
> Why is Kevin going home earlier today? – Maybe he is expecting visitors.

a) Oliver never watches videos.

b) Sam is very tired today.

c) Sue needs change.

d) Mrs Tyler has not spoken to her husband for two days.

e) Many people do not like going to Mary Jenkins.

f) Gary is in hospital.

Negotiating games

2 Players

19 Optimist and pessimist

Level 3

20 min.

Player A

1. *You have a positive outlook on people and life. You always expect the best. Here are a few things that have happened or will happen to you. Discuss with B.*

> *Example:*
>
> A mutual friend wants to come and stay over Christmas.
>
> *As an optimist, you could say, for instance:*
>
> I'm really looking forward to his visit. I'm sure we will have a lot of fun. He's a nice person. I expect he'll bring a lovely/super/great present.

a) A mutual friend is going to the Casino tonight.

b) B is going to the doctor's for a routine check-up tomorrow.

c) You are getting married in three months.

d) Two police officers want to speak to your teacher.

e) A young family with three small children has just moved in next to B.

f) You are going on holiday next week.

2. *Now change roles. You have a negative outlook on people and life. You always expect the worst. Talk to B about the following:*

> *Example:*
>
> A mutual friend wants to come and stay over Christmas.
>
> *As a pessimist you might say:*
>
> I don't think it is a good idea at all. It will probably be awfully boring. I think he's a strange person. And he probably won't bring a single present.

g) Two mutual friends are going on a mountain tour.

h) A mutual friend has just had a baby.

i) B answered a job ad in the paper. He's going for an interview.

j) You are having a big party tomorrow evening.

k) A mutual friend has just won the jackpot.

l) B is going on holiday in two weeks.

Negotiating games

19 Optimist and pessimist

Player B

1. *You have a negative outlook on people and life. You always expect the worst. Here are a few things that have happened or will happen to you. Talk to A about the following:*

> *Example:*
> A mutual friend wants to come and stay over Christmas.
>
> *As a pessimist you might say:*
> I don't think it is a good idea at all. It will probably be awfully boring. I think he's a strange person. And he probably won't bring a single present.

a) A mutual friend is going to the Casino tonight.
b) You are going to the doctor's for a routine check-up tomorrow.
c) A is getting married in three months.
d) Two police officers want to speak to your teacher.
e) A young family with three small children has just moved in next to you.
f) A is going on holiday next week.

2. *Now change roles. You now have a positive outlook on people and life. You always expect the best. Discuss the following with A:*

> *Example:*
> A mutual friend wants to come and stay over Christmas.
>
> *As an optimist, you could say, for instance:*
> I'm really looking forward to his visit. I'm sure we will have a lot of fun. He's a nice person. I expect he'll bring a lovely/super/great present.

g) Two mutual friends are going on a mountain tour.
h) A mutual friend has just had a baby.
i) You answered a job ad in the paper. You are going for an interview.
j) A is having a big party tomorrow evening.
k) A mutual friend has just won the jackpot.
l) You are going on holiday in two weeks.

Negotiating games

3 Players

Level 2

30 min.

20 Let's spend Saturday together

Player A

You would like to spend your Saturday with B and C. These are your plans:

– You would like to spend the day at the seaside, sunbathing, reading and playing cards.
– You would like to have a picnic lunch. Tell the others what food you would bring.
– And in the evening, you would like to have a big party in the garden. Tell the others who you would like to invite.

Try and convince the others to do the same thing.

> I have an idea: …
> I think we ought to …
> I would like to …
> We could …
> How about …
> Why don't we …

Player B

You would like to spend your Saturday with A and C. These are your plans:

– You would like to get up early and go for a walking tour.
– You would like to have a picnic lunch. Tell the others what food you would bring.
– In the evening, you would like to go to the cinema and then on to a disco. Tell the others which film you would like to see.

Try and convince the others to do the same thing.

> I have an idea: …
> I think we ought to …
> I would like to …
> We could …
> How about …
> Why don't we …

20 Let's spend Saturday together

Player C

You would like to spend your Saturday with A and B. These are your plans:

- You would like to invite A and B for breakfast and you would then like to go shopping with them.
- You would like to grab a sandwich for lunch and then go and visit a mutual friend.
- In the evening, you would like to go to a very good restaurant. Tell the others which restaurant it is and what specialities they serve.

Try and convince the others to do the same thing.

> I have an idea: …
> I think we ought to …
> I would like to …
> We could …
> How about …
> Why don't we …

Board games
Snakes and ladders

Snakes and ladders are competitive games for small groups of 3 to 5 players.

You will need: one piece per player, a die and matches.

Snakes and ladders rules:

All players place their pieces on Start.

The first player throws the die and moves his piece onto the square. He then has to accomplish the task. If he does, he gets a match. If he doesn't, he must move back one square. If the square is at the foot of a ladder, he has to move back another 2 squares. If he lands on a snake's head while moving back, he has to slide down the ladder.

Then it's the next player's turn.

General rule: if a piece lands on a square with the foot of a ladder, go up the ladder.
If you land on a square with a snake's head, slide down to the end of the snake.

There are two winners: the lucky one who reaches Finish first, and the expert who got the most matches.

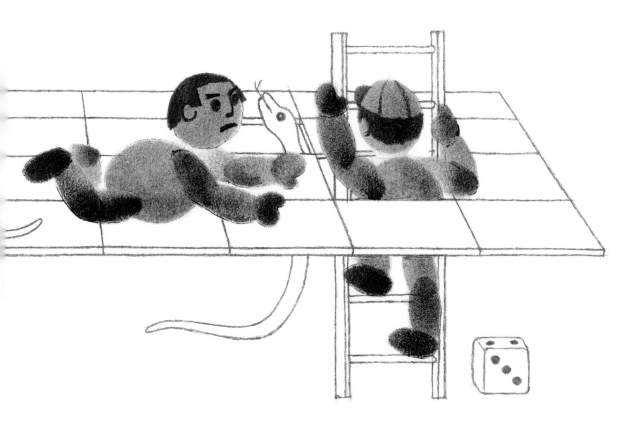

Board games · Snakes and ladders

21 In a restaurant

3-5 Players

1 Piece per player

1 Die

Matches

Level 2

45 min.

▶ See page 49 for rules

Board games · Snakes and ladders

START ⇧

1	The waiter brought you strawberries and cream, but the cream isn't fresh.
2	You would like to order.
3	You would like a small ice cream for your child. You don't know if this is possible.
4	You want to have the menu.
5	Your soup is cold. What do you say to the waiter?
6	You are with your child in the restaurant. You would like one portion of spaghetti with two plates.
7	You don't want anything to eat, just a drink.
8	You would like to sit at a table near the window.
9	You got your coffee, but no sugar.
10	You got a bottle of wine without a glass.
11	You would like a steak. You would rather have salad than potatoes.
12	The waiter brought you a warm beer.
13	You would like to pay by credit card.
14	You order a starter and a main course.
15	Your cutlet came without a knife.
16	You would rather have Yorkshire pudding than roast potatoes with the roast beef.
17	You are sitting in a non smoking zone, but the man next to you is smoking a huge cigar.
18	You would like to use the phone.
19	You don't know what to eat and ask the waiter to suggest something.
20	Your soup has come without a spoon.
21	You need some salt.
22	You have paid but you need a receipt.
23	You would like to pay and ask for the bill.
24	You want to order a sweet so you ask for the menu.
25	You order a sweet.
26	You pay your bill and ask the waiter for some change in order to use the phone.

FINISH

Board games · Snakes and ladders

22 Could I ...?

3-5 Players

1 Piece per player

1 Die

Matches

Level 2

30 min.

▶ See page 49 for rules

Can I ...?
Could I ... possibly?
Do you mind if I ...?
Would you mind if I ...?

Can you ...?
Could you ...?
Would you mind ...-ing ...?

Example:
Would you mind opening the window?

Board games · Snakes and ladders

Someone has brought some chocolate and you would like to try some.	You are going on holiday for 2 weeks but you can't take your dog.	It's cold and the window is open.	It's hot and the window is shut.		**FINISH**
You want to go camping at the weekend but you have no tent.	You don't feel very well. You need a glass of water.		You want to make notes of something but you don't have a pen.	You are ill and can't come to the English lesson. Ask another student to inform your teacher.	Your teacher speaks very fast and you can't understand.
You are at a friend's house and have to make a phone call.	In the pub, you would like to buy the next round.	You need to leave the room. Ask another student to look after your things.	You are at lunch and you need the salt.		You phone Mrs Green and her secretary answers.
Your are cooking and you need an egg. Go and ask your neighbour.	Ask another student for his phone number.	You need a piece of paper but you don't have any.	You must mail an urgent letter but have no time to go to the letter box.	Your homework is very difficult. You can't manage alone.	Someone told you about a very good book. You would like to borrow it.
⬇	At the bank, you would like to change 500 marks into pounds.	You are having coffee and you need sugar.	You need 30p to make a phone call but you have no change.		Your neighbours are playing very loud music. You would like them to turn it down.
START ⬆	You would like to get a coffee out of the vending machine but you have no change.				

Board games · Snakes and ladders

3-5 Players

1 Piece per player

1 Die

Matches

Level 3

20 min.

23 Spot the preposition

▶ See page 49 for rules

Match a preposition to a verb and form a sentence. The player receives a match only when he has formed a grammatically correct *and* meaningful sentence.

Variation:
Depending on students' level, the sentences can be formed in the present or the present perfect.

Example:
You should tidy up your room.

The following prepositions are needed:
up, down, out, into, in, on, off, across, from, after

Board games · Snakes and ladders

FINISH	come	climb	lie	stay
	grow		stand	come
turn ⇧		get ⇧	lock ⇩	run
throw	hold	keep	key	walk
	hurry ⇩		send	⇧
turn ⇧	carry	stand ⇧	look ⇩	slip
speak	drop	go	hear	START ⇧

55

Board games · Snakes and ladders

3-5 Players

1 Piece per player

1 Die

Matches

Level 2

30 min.

24 Fill the gaps

▶ See page 49 for rules

Players should complete the sentences with: for, since, ago.
Or they should put the verbs in the right tense. The player receives a match only when he has formed a grammatically correct *and* meaningful sentence.

Example:
I lived in London 4 years ago.

Board games · Snakes and ladders

He hasn't written ... 6 weeks.	I ... here since Monday. (be)	He left 6 weeks	I ... here for one year. (work)	They ... with us since Easter. (stay)	**FINISH**
She has been living here ... 1986.	I ... for one hour. (wait)	I ... lunch an hour ago. (have)			I haven't seen him ... 10 months.
I haven't had anything to eat ... this morning.	I ... to London two months ago. (go)	Three years ..., I visited Norway.	They have known each other ... two years.	We ... English for a long time. (learn)	I have been playing the piano ... I ... (be) a child.
We met three years	I have been on a diet ... three weeks.	He ... Germany a long time ago. (leave)	We ... this game for twenty minutes now. (play)	The war continued ... 3 years.	He stopped smoking two weeks ... .
START	He has been married ... six years.		We ... in front of this shop for quite some time now. (stand)	She hasn't had a Chinese meal ... she was ill.	I lived in Edinburgh ... 6 years.

Dice and board games

These games should be played in small groups of three to six players.

Rules
All players place their pieces on a square of their choice. If pieces are not available, coins can be used. The players then throw the die in turn and can move in either direction.
As there is no start or finish, a time limit should be set. (Between 20 and 45 minutes, depending on the number of players).

Cooperative games:
One die and one piece per player are needed.

Competitive games:
One die, one piece per player and matches are needed. The player who has the most matches at the end of the game is the winner.

Dice and board games

3-6 Players

1 Piece per player

1 Die

Level 3

45 min.

25 Dreams and wishes

▶ See page 59 for rules

The first player throws the die and moves his piece on to the appropriate square.

He then expresses a wish or dream concerning the subject mentioned on the square. Then the next player does the same thing, and so on.

If a player lands on the same square a second time, he can pass the question to another player.

Examples:

I would like to be a famous painter.
I would like to go to Italy on holiday.
If I had more money I would move into a larger flat.

I wish	I could play the piano.
	I didn't have to work so hard.
	I had more time to go to the cinema.

Dice and board games

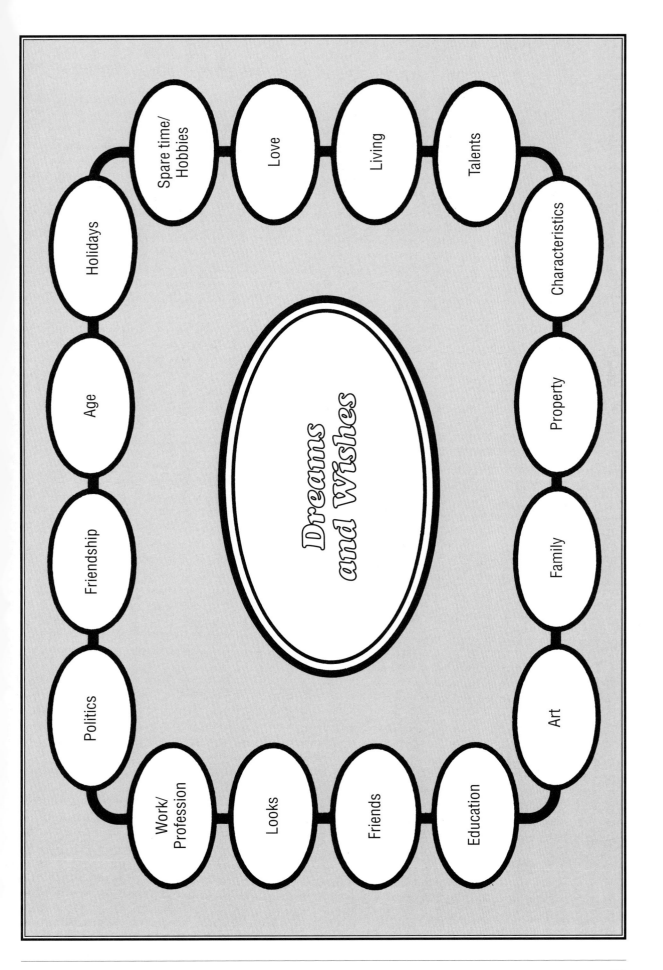

Dice and board games

3-6 Players

26 Who says what?

1 Piece per player

▶ See page 59 for rules

The first player throws the die and moves his piece to the appropriate square. After having read the text, he describes a situation in which this text could appear. As an alternative, he can think of a dialogue where the text would appear at the end.

1 Die

Then it is the next player's turn.

If a player lands on the same square a second time, he will have to think of another situation or dialogue.

Level 2

30 min.

Dice and board games

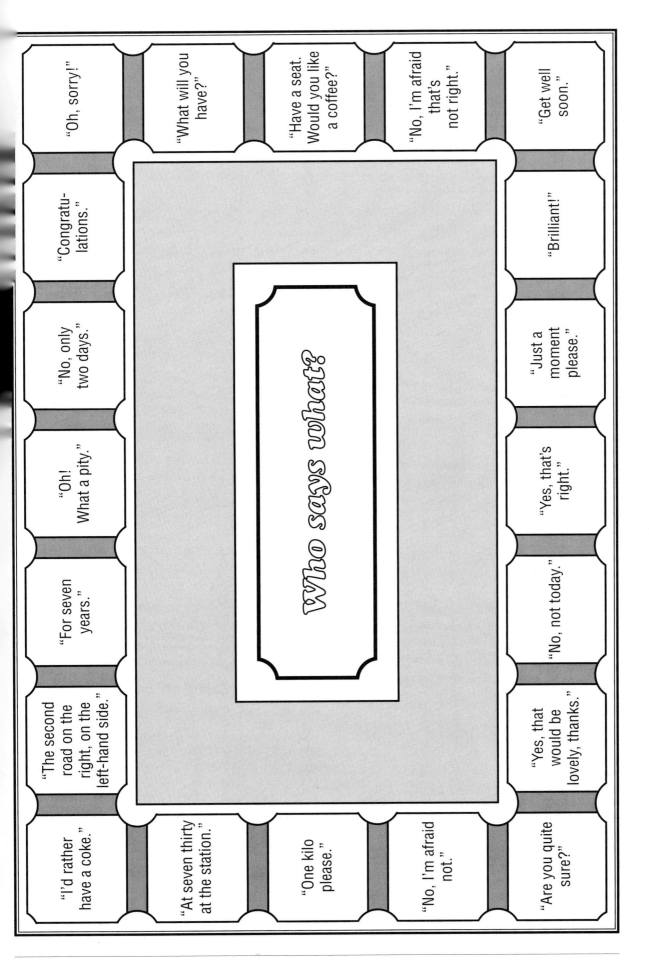

Dice and board games

3-6 Players

27 *How often? – When? – How long?*

1 Piece per player

▶ See page 59 for rules

You will need pencils and paper for this game.

1 Die

The first player throws the die and moves his piece onto the appropriate square. He then asks his neighbour a question with one of the following: *How often? When? How long?* depending on which makes the most sense. The neighbour writes his answer on a piece of paper without showing it. The player then has to guess what his neighbour has written. He has two goes.

If his guess is right, the neighbour has to give him a match. If his guess is wrong, he has to give his neighbour a match.

10 Matches per player

After this, the second player throws the die.
A time limit should be set. If a player has lost all his matches before the end, he cannot play any more.

Pen and paper

How often?
every day / every year   never
once a day/week/month

Level 1

When?
at ten – at about four thirty – between eight and nine o'clock
in the morning/evening/afternoon – at night
on Mondays/Tuesdays etc.
in January/May – in summer/winter

45 min.

How long?
about three minutes
roughly half an hour

Dice and board games

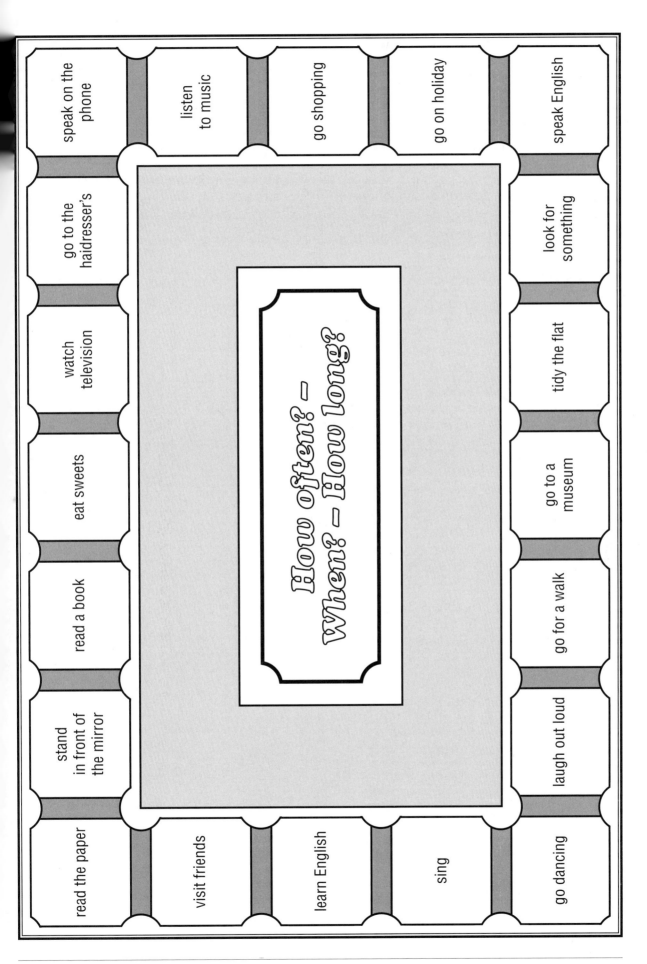

How often? – When? – How long?

- speak on the phone
- listen to music
- go shopping
- go on holiday
- speak English
- look for something
- tidy the flat
- go to a museum
- go for a walk
- laugh out loud
- go dancing
- sing
- learn English
- visit friends
- read the paper
- stand in front of the mirror
- read a book
- eat sweets
- watch television
- go to the hairdresser's

Dice and board games

3-6 Players

28 What do you prefer?

1 Piece per player

▶ See page 59 for rules

You will need pencils and paper for this game.

1 Die

The first player throws the die and moves his piece onto the appropriate square. He then asks his neighbour the completed question. The neighbour writes his answer on a piece of paper without showing it. The player then has to guess what his neighbour has written.

If his guess is right, the neighbour has to give him a match. If his guess is wrong, he has to give his neighbour a match.

10 Matches per player

After this, the second player throws the die.

A time limit should be set. If a player has lost all his matches before the end, he cannot play any more.

Pen and paper

What do you think is more interesting: reading or watching TV?
What do you prefer: books or films?
I think reading is more interesting than watching TV.
In my opinion books are more interesting than films.
I prefer books to films.
I am more interested in books than in films.

Level 2

45 min.

66

Dice and board games

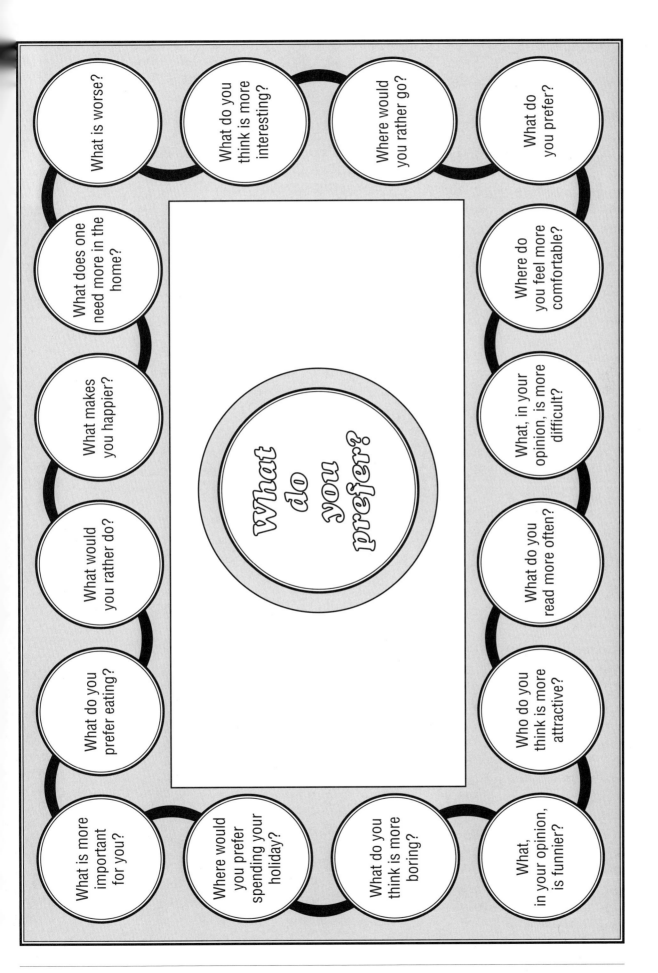

67

Dice and board games

3-6 Players

29 Comparing

1 Piece per player

▶ See page 59 for rules

The first player throws the die and moves to the appropriate square. He then compares the two words. The other players can ask him to give his reasons. Those who disagree have to say why. The player gets a match if the majority agrees.

1 Die

Then the next player throws the die.

Matches

> In my opinion, reading is more interesting than watching TV.
> I think reading is just as interesting as watching TV.
> I prefer reading to watching TV because … .
> I'd rather read than watch TV because … .
> I don't think reading is as interesting as watching TV because … .

Level 2

45 min.

Dice and board games

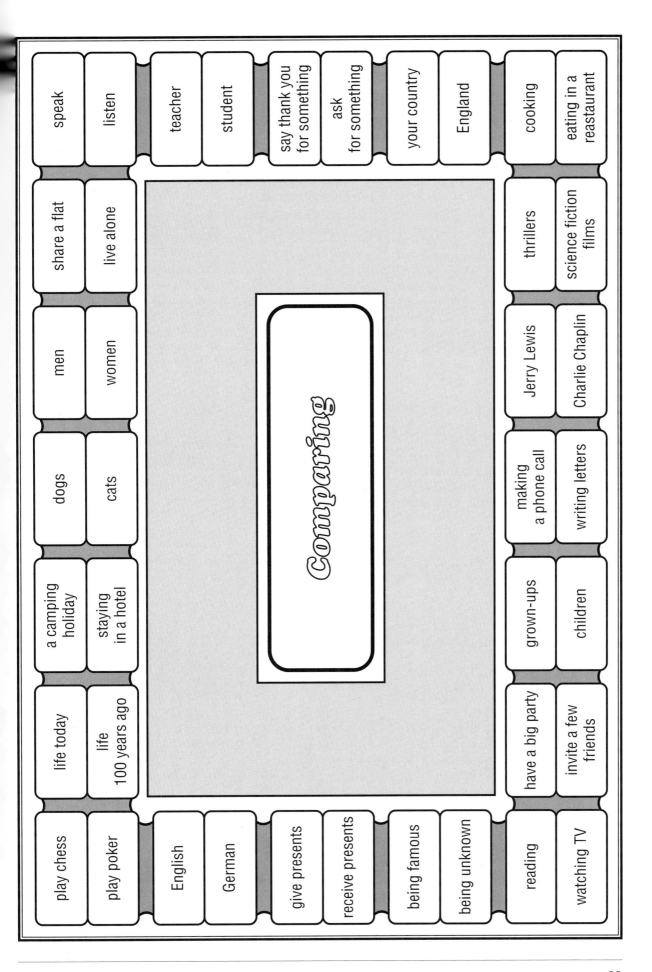

Dice and board games

3-6 Players

30 Opinion survey

1 Piece per player

▶ See page 59 for rules

1 Die

You will need pencil and paper for this game.

The first player throws the die, moves his piece to the appropriate square and reads out the sentence. He now has to guess how many players will agree with this statement and make a note of his guess. He then asks who agrees within the group. If his guess was right, he gets a match.

Then it's the next player's turn.

Matches

> I think one of you/none of you believes that one should not lie.
> I suppose two/three of you think one should not lie.
> Who thinks/believes that one shouldn't lie?

Pen and paper

Level 2

60 min.

Dice and board games

Opinion survey

- Women are more sensitive than men.
- Good looking people have an easier life.
- One needs to punish children sometimes.
- There are intelligent beings on other planets.
- Men are more intelligent than women.
- All people are selfish.
- In a hundred years from now the earth will be destroyed.
- Women wear make-up for men.
- Money makes you happy.
- A man can bring up children just as well as a woman.
- One should never lie.
- Exercise is good for you.
- Children are not well accepted in Germany.
- All people are basically good.
- Most politicians are corrupt.
- All mothers love their children.
- There is life after death.
- Mothers with small children should not go out to work.
- Life is wonderful.
- Life used to be better.

Dice and board games

3-6 Players

31 Where would I use it?

▶ See page 59 for rules

1 Piece per player

You will need one white and one black die.

Each player places his piece on a square of the outer circle.

2 Dice

The first player throws both dice. The white dice stays on the outer circle and moves according to the number shown on the dice. The player places the black dice on the corresponding number in the inner square. The player has to tell the group how he would use the object in that particular place. The other players can ask him for his reasons if his suggestion is not clear. Then the players vote. Those who do not accept his suggestion must say why. If the majority accepts the player's suggestion, he gets a match and then it's the next player's turn.

Matches

Level 3

With one pound I can/could buy an ice-cream on holiday.
I can/could/would use a pound to buy an ice-cream on holiday.
I use a pen at school if I want to write something.
I would use a knife in the kitchen if I wanted to cut something.

45 min.

72

Dice and board games

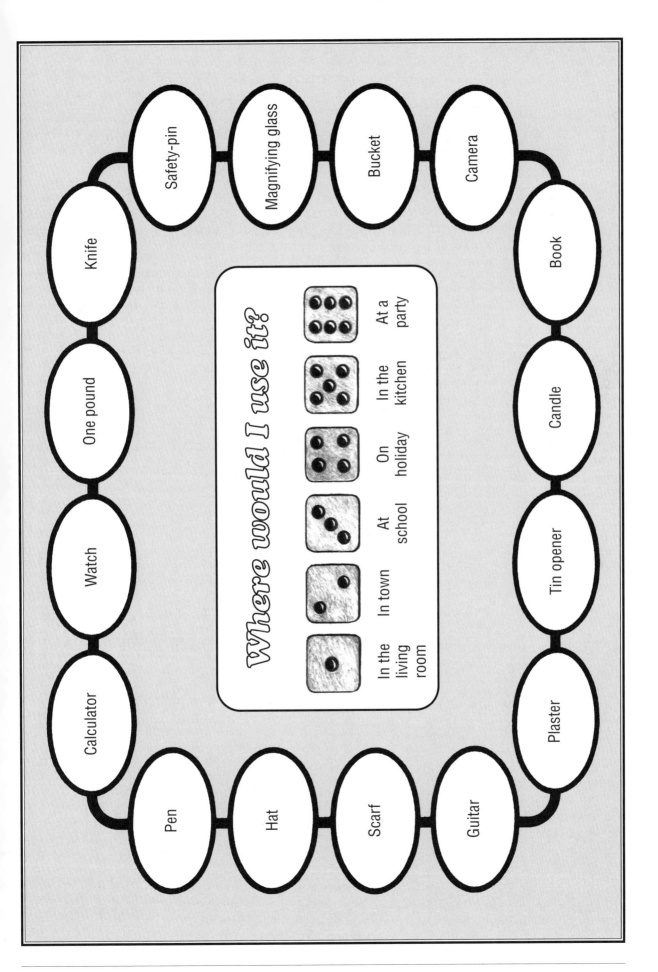

73

Dice and board games

3-6 Players

32 The clock

▶ See page 59 for rules

1 Piece per player

Each player needs pen and paper.

Put all pieces on the centre of the clock.

1 Die

The first to throw a six starts from the circled 12 o'clock. He throws the dice again and moves in any direction. He can jump between the inner and outer circle. Once he has landed on a time (e.g. 14.30) he should think of a day of the week. He then asks another player a question: e.g. *What do I normally do on Sundays at 14.30?*

Matches

All players write down their answers without showing them. They then read them out and those who had the same answer as the player whose turn it was get a match.

The next player then also starts at 12 o'clock.

Pen and paper

What do you think I usually do on Mondays at 16.30/4.30 in the afternoon/4.30 p.m.?
What do I do on Friday evenings at 8 o'clock?

Well, I think you …
You probably …

Level 1

20 min.

Dice and board games

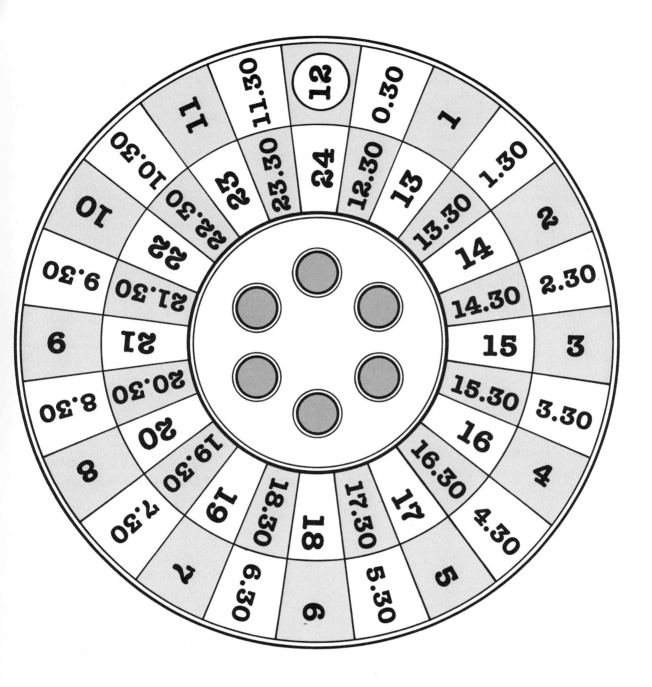

Dice and board games

3-6 Players

33 Comparatives and superlatives

1 Die

Matches

Pen and paper

Level 2

30 min.

The group decides how long the game will last (20 to 45 minutes according to the number of players).

The first player rolls the die. Say a six is thrown he choses a word from column six. He then asks the other players for example: *What is difficult to learn? What book is boring?*

All players then have 15 seconds to write an answer on a slip of paper without showing it to the others. Any player who can't think of an answer should skip the round.

Players read their answers to the group and compare them (see examples). The group decides who had the best answer and that player gets a match. Then the next player rolls the die and the game continues.

The winner is the player who got the most matches.

Examples:

I	think believe	cars are faster than horses. German is more difficult than English. sailing is more exciting than surfing.
In my opinion		a bar stool is the most uncomfortable place to sit. car racing is the most dangerous sport. water is the best drink.

Dice and board games

⚅	difficult	useful	easy	clever	cheap	fast
⚄	boring	bad	good	expensive	nice	tall
⚃	hard	uncomfortable	beautiful	young	famous	little
⚂	far	old	terrible	dangerous	quiet	easy
⚁	exciting	attractive	light	slow	sweet	big

77

Dice and board games

3-6 Players

34 Vocabulary board

1 Die

The first player throws the dice and chooses a question from the corresponding list.

The other players have two minutes to write down as many words (not sentences) as possible. Each player then reads out his list. Other players should feel free to object and discuss. The majority decides. The player with the most words gets a match and goes next.

Matches

The questions can only be used once. If all the question in the list have been asked, or if the player throws a six *(Joker)*, he can choose any other remaining question.

The winner is the player who has the most matches at the end of the game.

Pen and paper

Level 1

60 min.

Dice and board games

	Humans and animals	Indoors and outdoors	Activities	Personal things	General	Joker
⚀	Which parts of the body do you know?	What is in the kitchen?	What does a housewife do?	What do you wish for yourself?	What is bad for you?	
⚁	Who do you speak to often?	What is in the living room?	What does one do at school?	Where do you not like to be?	What is good for you?	
⚂	What do people look like?	What can one see in a town?	What can one play?	Where do you like to be?	What can one hear?	
⚃	Which animals do you know?	Where can you buy something?	What can one do at a party?	What do you find terrible?	What can't one see?	
⚄	Which professions do you know?	What can one see in the country?	What hobbies do you know?	What do you enjoy?	What is round?	
⚅	Where do people work?	What can you find on holiday?	What do most people do?	What is your best friend/partner like?	What can one celebrate?	

79

Dialogue games

These information gap activities are for students working in pairs.
Instructions are given for student A and student B.

Dialogue games

35 Let's go to London

2 Players

Level 1

30 min.

Student A

Start by reading 1. Then listen to what B answers and then choose the right answer from 3. Continue in the same way until the end of the dialogue.

1 A: Hello … How are you?
2 B:
3 A   a) I'm sorry to hear that. What is the matter with him?
     b) Oh dear, what's wrong? Aren't you feeling well?
     c) Fine thanks. Are you doing anything on Wednesday?
4 B
5 A: a) I'm going to London. Would you like to come too?
     b) We are fine. By the way, we're going to Brighton on Saturday, why don't you come with us.
     c) I'm fine. Tell me, are you free on Wednesday?
6 B:
7 A: a) I'm driving up to York at about 11 o'clock. Would you like to come with me?
     b) I'd like to leave as early as possible, say, about 8 o'clock. Is that OK?
     c) Oh, that doesn't matter, just bring them along.
8 B:
9 A: a) What a pity. Oh well, never mind. See you soon.
     b) No, I'll pick you up at your home. See you then.
     c) At my place, if that's OK.

Student B

Listen to what A tells you, then choose the right answer from 2. Continue in the same way until the end of the dialogue.

1 A:
2 B: a) Not so well I'm afraid.
     b) Oh, I'm very well thanks, and you?
     c) Well, alright. My son is not very well though.
3 A:
4 B: a) I don't think so, why?
     b) I think I've got a virus, but how are you?
     c) He's got the flu. How are you, and how's the family?
5 A:
6 B: a) Yes, I am, why?
     b) I'd love to. When do you want to leave?
     c) I'm afraid I can't make it on Saturday. My parents-in-law are coming to stay.
7 A:
8 B: a) Yes, that's fine. Where shall we meet?
     b) No, I'm afraid that's not a very good idea. They get car sick, you see.
     c) Yes, I'd love to. See you at your house at eleven, then.
9 A:

Dialogue games

36 Meeting a friend

2 Players

Level 2

25 min.

Student A

Start by reading 1. Then listen to what B answers and then choose the right answer from 3. Continue in the same way until the end of the dialogue.

1 A: Good morning ..., how are you? I haven't seen you for a long time. Have you been ill?
2 B:
3 A: a) Oh, I'm sorry to hear that. Are you a bit better now?
    b) That's nice. Where did you go?
    c) I'm sure you did. Are they still here?
4 B:
5 A: a) And what was the weather like? Did you have a lot of rain too?
    b) Fine, thanks. Let's have a coffee or are you in a hurry ?
    c) Well, why don't you come to our house for a drink. Let's say, on Saturday?
6 B:
7 A: a) Should we go to the tea shop over there? They've got delicious cakes.
    b) Yes, I can see, you have a lovely tan. Well, I've got to go. Give my love to your wife/husband/children.
    c) What a shame. Well, another time then. I'll give you a ring.
8 B:

Student B

Listen to what A tells you, then choose the right answer from 2. Continue in the same way until the end of the dialogue.

1 A:
2 B: a) No, we've been on holiday. We only came back yesterday.
    b) No, not at all. My parents-in-law were here. I've had a lot to do.
    c) Yes. Unfortunately, I have had a very bad cold. I was in bed for two weeks.
3 A:
4 B: a) No, they left last Monday. I can relax now.
    b) Yes, much better, thank goodness. And how are you?
    c) Well, first we went over to Holland and then drove down through France.
5 A:
6 B: a) Oh, I'm afraid we won't be able to come on Saturday. We are going to Scotland for the weekend.
    b) No, not at all. It was great. We went to the beach every day.
    c) Good idea. Where shall we go?
7 A:
8 B: a) Yes I will. Give ... my love, too. Bye.
    b) That would be lovely. I'll see you soon, then.
    c) Fine. Let's go then.

Dialogue games

37 My neighbour's groceries

2 Players

Level 1

20 min.

Student A

1. You are cooking a meal. You need the following but you don't have any. Ask your partner for them.

| Excuse me, | have you got some salt? |
| | a couple of eggs? |

Sorry, but could you give me some milk?

I only need	a bit of butter.
	a spoon of sugar.
	a cup of milk.
	about 100 grams of flour.
	2 rolls.

2. Student B needs some groceries. You have these:

Yes, how much milk do you need?
How many eggs do you want?
I'm sorry but I don't have any cheese/jam either.
I'm afraid I don't have any bread either.

Dialogue games

37 My neighbour's groceries

Student B

1. Student A needs a few groceries and asks you for them. You have these:

> Yes, how much milk do you need?
> How many eggs do you want?
> I'm sorry but I don't have any cheese/jam either.
> I'm afraid I don't have any bread either.

2. You are cooking a meal. You need the following but you don't have any. Ask your partner for them.

| Excuse me, | have you got some salt? |
| | a couple of eggs? |

Sorry, but could you give me some milk?

I only need	a bit of butter.
	a spoon of sugar.
	a cup of milk.
	about 100 grams of flour.
	2 rolls.

Dialogue games

2 Players

38 Which present?

Level 2

Student A

1. *Christmas is not far away and you don't know which presents to get. Ask your partner to help you.*

30 min.

Example:

Colleague – likes cooking

A: Have you any idea what I could give my colleague for Christmas?
B: Is there anything he/she particularly likes?
A: Cooking, I think. / I think he/she likes to cook.
B: Well, why don't you give him/her a cookery book.
A: Good idea. That is what I'll get him/her.

You want to buy presents for the following people:

a) Neighbour – likes reading

b) Mother – likes writing letters

c) Aunt and Uncle – music lovers

d) Grandfather – likes reading but doesn't see too well

e) Brother – likes painting

f) Girlfriend – is having a baby in four months

g) Niece – would like a bicycle, but is still too young

h) Boyfriend/Girlfriend – you would like to marry him/her soon

2. *B is now going to ask you for your advice. These are the presents he could get.*

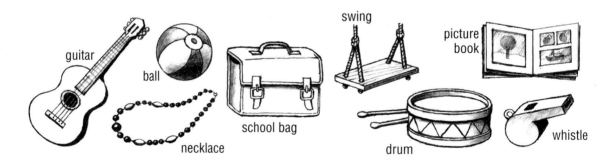

86

38 Which present?

Student B

1. Christmas is not far away. A would like to get some presents. Give him your advice.

> *Example:*
>
> Colleague – likes cooking
>
> A: Have you any idea what I could give my colleague for Christmas?
> B: Is there anything he/she particularly likes?
> A: Cooking, I think. / I think he/she likes to cook.
> B: Well, why don't you give him/her a cookery book.
> A: Good idea. That is what I'll get him/her.

These are the presents A could get:

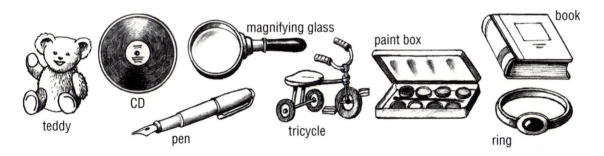

2. You would also like to buy some presents, but what? Ask your partner for his advice.

You want to buy presents for the following people:

a) Nephews – five and seven – like playing together

b) Sister-in-law – likes jewelry

c) Daughter and son – like playing in the garden

d) Neighbour's child – likes making noise

e) Friend – referee in a football club in his spare time

f) Girlfriend – would like to play an instrument

g) Sister – starting school next year

h) Brother – likes books, can't read yet

Dialogue games

39 Where can I go?

2 Players

Level 1

25 min.

Student A

1. *You have just arrived in England and you have some wishes and wants. Tell your partner about them and he will tell you where to go.*

| I | need ...
have ...
would like ...
must ... | What should I do/can I do?
What can you suggest?
Where do you think I should go? |

a) You haven't got any more cash, just cheques.
b) You would like to go for a good meal.
c) You would like some information on interesting English towns.
d) You need some stamps.
e) You would like to go dancing.
f) You have a bad flu.
g) You can't find a place to park.
h) You would like to go swimming.
i) You are interested in English literature.
j) You would like to go for a walk.
k) You would like to have a cheeseburger.

2. *Now swap roles. Your partner will tell you about his wishes and wants. Tell him where he can go.*

Go to ...
You can go to ...
Why don't you go to ...

the bank	the restaurant	the tourist office
the garage	the café	the swimming-pool
the post office	the station	the park
the take-away	the golf course	the doctor
the tennis court	the market	the museum
the library	the disco	the dentist

88

39 Where can I go?

Student B

1. *A has just arrived in England and tells you about his wishes and wants. Tell him where to go.*

> Go to …
> You can go to …
> Why don't you go to …

the bank	the restaurant	the tourist office
the garage	the café	the swimming-pool
the post office	the station	the park
the take-away	the golf course	the doctor
the tennis court	the market	the museum
the library	the disco	the dentist

2. *Now swap roles. Your partner will tell you about his wishes and problems. Tell him where he can go.*

> I need …
> have …
> would like …
> must …
>
> What should I do/can I do?
> What can you suggest?
> Where do you think I should go?

a) You need a ticket.

b) You would like a piece of cake.

c) You would like to meet people.

d) You need to send a telegram.

e) You would like to see another town at the weekend.

f) You need to change some money.

g) You have a toothache.

h) You are interested in art.

i) You would like to sunbathe.

j) You would like to have a cheap meal.

k) You would like to buy fresh vegetables.

Dialogue games

2 Players

40 Can you help me?

Level 2

Student A

45 min.

1. *Your partner will ask you a few things. Help him if you can. If you can't, tell him why. First read the information below and then listen to what your partner wants.*

> I'm sorry/afraid I can't help you because …
> I can't help you because …

a) You have left your dictionary at home.

b) You are a stranger in this town.

c) You have a lot of change.

d) You don't know any doctor here. But you have just bought some cough sweets.

e) Your pen is broken but you have a pencil.

f) You are not going home after the English class. You are going to the cinema.

2. *Now ask your partner to help you.*

> Could you please …?
> I wonder if you could …?
> Can you please …?
> Can I …?
> May I …?

a) You have lost a contact lense and can't find it.

b) You would like to go shopping after class but you have left your money at home.

c) You have a cold but you don't have a handkerchief.

d) You are going on holiday next week. Perhaps your partner could water your plants.

e) Your partner has an interesting book. You would like to read it.

f) You need a baby-sitter for this evening.

Dialogue games

40 Can you help me?

Student B

1. *Ask your partner to help you.*

> Could you please …?
> I wonder if you could …?
> Can you please …?
> Can I …?
> May I …?

a) You would like to borrow your partner's dictionary.

b) You would like to know where the post office is.

c) You have a pound note and need change.

d) You have a terrible cough. Maybe your partner knows a good doctor.

e) You would like to borrow your partner's pen.

f) You would like your partner to drive you home after the English class.

2. *Now your partner will ask you a few things. Help him if you can. If you can't, tell him why. First read the information below and then listen to what your partner wants.*

> I'm sorry/afraid I can't help you because …
> I can't help you because …

a) You have left your glasses at home so you can't see very well.

b) You have got five pounds in your wallet.

c) You have just bought a pack of handkerchiefs.

d) You are going away next week but you sister will be here.

e) You have taken the book out from the library. You have to take it back the day after tomorrow.

f) You are going to a concert this evening.

Dialogue games

41 Excuse me, but ...

2 Players

Level 2

30 min.

Student A

1. *Complain to your partner about the following situations.*

> Excuse me, but ...
> Could/Would you please ...?
> Do you think you could ...?

a) You are in a taxi. The driver is going too fast. You are afraid.

b) Your partner is writing something on the blackboard. His writing is so bad that you can't read it.

c) Your partner is speaking too fast. You can hardly understand him.

d) You play tennis with your partner once a week. He is always late. This makes you angry.

e) Your neighbour listens to very loud music every night. This disturbs you.

f) You share an office with your partner who always wears very strong perfume. This gives you a headache.

g) You are in a shop. There are a few people in front of you but now your partner tries to jump the queue.

2. *Your partner complains to you about the following. Answer politely.*

> Oh, I'm sorry, I didn't realise ...
> Excuse me, I didn't know ...

a) You are talking to your partner.

b) You don't have a garage and this is why you park in front of the house.

c) You have a dog. He's a bit crazy but quite harmless. He sometimes plays outside.

d) You like to watch TV in the evening. You are a little deaf.

e) You share an office with your partner. You smoke.

f) You have just bought a piano and like to practise for hours.

g) You are at the theatre. The play is just starting.

41 Excuse me, but ...

Student B

1. *Your partner complains to you about the following. Answer politely.*

> Oh, I'm sorry, I didn't realise ...
> Excuse me, I didn't know ...

a) You are a taxi driver. Your partner is sitting in your taxi.
b) You are writing something on the board.
c) You are talking to your partner.
d) You play tennis with your partner once a week. He is usually there before you.
e) You love music and listen to it nearly every evening.
f) You share an office with your partner. You love wearing perfume.
g) You are in a shop. You think it's your turn now.

2. *Complain to your partner about the following situations.*

> Excuse me, but ...
> Could/Would you please ...?
> Do you think you could ...?

a) Your partner speaks too softly. You can hardly understand him.
b) Your partner – who is also your neighbour – always parks his car almost in front of your garage. You find it difficult to drive in and out.
c) Your partner/neighbour has a large dog. The dog is often running loose. The dog seems aggressive and you are afraid.
d) Your neighbour turns his TV up very loud. You can hear it every evening.
e) You share an office with your partner. He is a heavy smoker. This bothers you.
f) Your partner plays the piano a lot. You would like to have an afternoon nap.
g) You go to the theatre. You have seat number 32. Your partner is sitting on your seat.

Dialogue games

42 Don't worry ...

2 Players

Level 2

30 min.

Student A

1. *The following little accidents have happened to you. Apologise to your partner.*

> I'm afraid I ...
> I'm very/terribly/awfully sorry, but ...
> I've done a silly thing: I ... . I do apologise.

a) B lent you a glass bowl. It fell on the floor and broke.

b) You sat on B's cigarette pack and now all the cigarettes are broken.

c) B lent you an umbrella and you left it on the train.

d) B lent you a book and a child drew in it.

e) Yesterday you wanted to post a letter for B but you forgot.

f) B lent you a pullover. You washed it and now it has shrunk.

g) You wanted to bring B a video cassette but you forgot.

h) You promised to baby-sit for B but now you can't. Give reasons.

2. *B apologises. Tell him not to worry.*

> Don't worry, it's not so/that bad.
> It doesn't matter.
> It could happen to anybody.

The following information will help you with your answers.

a) You lent B a CD. You don't like it.

b) You lent B some money. He wanted to give it back to you today. You have enough till the end of the month.

c) Your sofa is very old. You ordered a new one yesterday.

d) B went shopping for you. You have enough coffee.

e) You wanted to go away for the weekend and B was going to look after your cat. Now your car has broken down so you won't be going.

f) You lent B your bicycle. You would like to buy yourself a motor bike.

g) B wanted to get you some tickets for a concert. However, you know that the tickets are very expensive.

h) You are redecorating your flat at the weekend. Lots of friends have promised to help.

42   Don't worry …

Student B

1. *A apologises. Tell him not to worry.*

> Don't worry, it's not so/that bad.
> It doesn't matter.
> It could happen to anybody.

The following information will help you with your answers.

a) You lent A a glass bowl. You have a lot of bowls.
b) You smoke but you would like to give it up.
c) You lent A a very old umbrella.
d) You lent A a book. You have already read it and you didn't like it.
e) A wanted to mail a letter for you. You need to go to the post office today.
f) You lent A a pullover that didn't suit you.
g) A wanted to bring you a video cassette but your recorder is broken.
h) A promised to baby-sit for you tomorrow evening. You have cancelled your date.

2. *The following little accidents have happened to you. Apologise to your partner.*

> I'm afraid I …
> I'm very/terribly/awfully sorry, but …
> I've done a silly thing: I … . I do apologise.

a) A lent you a CD and you have lost it.
b) A lent you some money. You wanted to give it back today but you can't. Give reasons.
c) You have burnt a hole in A's sofa with your cigarette.
d) You went shopping for A but you forgot the coffee.
e) A wanted to go away for the weekend and you were going to look after his cat. Your landlord won't allow animals in the house.
f) A lent you his bicycle and it has been stolen.
g) You promised to get some concert tickets for A but you forgot. Now it is too late.
h) You promised to help A redecorate at the weekend. You can't come. Give reasons.

Dialogue games

2 Players

Level 2

25 min.

43 Make a suggestion

Student A

1. *You have a problem. Talk to B about it. He will make a suggestion.*

| I have a small problem:
I don't know what to do: | ... – | What do you suggest I should do about it?
What do you think? |

a) You have a headache.

b) You can't get to sleep at night.

c) You neighbour always plays loud music at night.

d) You have hiccups.

e) You have lost your wallet.

f) You are overworked.

g) You have lost your job.

h) You have a sunburn.

i) You live outside town. There are hardly any busses and no trains. You don't have a driving licence.

j) You bought a cassette player two days ago and it's broken.

2. *B tells you his problems. Make a suggestion.*

| I think you should/ought to ...
If I were you, I would ...
Why don't you ... |

do some yoga   look for a baby-sitter
take it to the cleaners   drink some hot lemon
talk to ...   go to the cinema
go to the police   take out a loan
go on a diet   use earphones

43 Make a suggestion

Student B

1. *A tells you his problems. Make a suggestion.*

> I think you should/ought to …
> If I were you, I would …
> Why don't you …

go to the job centre	drink a glass of water
go to the chemist	go on holiday
take it back	take a tablet
talk to …	go to the lost property office
go jogging in the evening	buy a bicycle

2. *You have a problem. Talk to B about it. He will make a suggestion.*

> I have a small problem: … – What do you suggest I should do about it?
> I don't know what to do: What do you think?

a) You would like to go out in the evenings but you have a small child.

b) You like to watch TV a lot but your husband/wife would like to read in the living room.

c) You would like to buy a car but you don't have enough money.

d) You have a bad cold.

e) You have put on 5 kilos on holiday.

f) There is a coffee stain on your silk blouse.

g) You have had an argument with your friend. Now he/she doesn't come and see you any more.

h) You are often very nervous.

i) A man has been following you for three days.

j) You are bored.

Dialogue games

2 Players

44 In the bookstore

Level 3

Student A

20 min.

With your partner act out a conversation in a bookstore. Here is some information for you.

- It is 5.15 p.m. You are in a bookstore. You would like a book on 17th century Chinese art.
- The sales person shows you a book and you like it very much.
- You have 50 pounds and no cheques but you do have a credit card.
- You live 30 minutes away.
- You definitely want to buy the book. You ask the sales person to reserve it for you till tomorrow.

Student B

With your partner act out a conversation in a bookstore. Here is some information for you.

- It is 5.15 p.m. You are a sales person in a bookstore. A customer would like a book on 17th century Chinese art.
- You show him a particularly interesting book on 16th and 17th century Chinese art.
- The book costs 67.50 pounds.
- Your shop accepts cheques but no credit cards.
- You shut at six.
- You can reserve books. However, the customer has to pay a deposit of 10%.

Key to the information gap games

Key to game 11: People in our street 1

	No. 1	No. 3	No. 5	No. 7	No. 9
Name	Joan French	Emma	Steven	Mrs Waters	Mr Winterbottom
Age	39	7	17	57	89
Profession	Police officer	Schoolgirl	Salesman	Doctor	Old age pensioner
Hobbies	Swimming	Riding the bike	Reading	No hobbies	Reading
Food/drink	Wine	Spaghetti	Meat	Coffee	Spaghetti

Key to game 12: People in our street 2

	No. 1	No. 3	No. 5	No. 7	No. 9
Name	Jean	Audrey Parker	Andrew Wright	Julia Richards	Fred Taylor
Marital status	Married	Single	Single or separated from his wife	Divorced	Widower
No. of children	2 daughters	1 daughter	1 son	–	2 sons
Profession	Housewife	Teacher	Bank manager	Hairdresser	Old age pensioner
Hobbies	Tennis	Reading	Swimming	Photography	Reading

Key to game 13: Family photo

Name	Charlotte	Joanne	Michael	Sophie	Paul	Steven
Relationship to others	Sophie's sister Steven's aunt Michael's great-aunt Joanne's mother	Charlotte's daughter Steven's cousin Sophie's niece	Paul's great-grandson Steven's son Sophie's grandson	Michael's grandmother Paul's daughter-in-law Charlotte's sister Joanne's aunt Steven's mother	Sophie's father-in-law Steven's grandfather Michael's great-grandfather	Paul's grandson Sophie's son Charlotte's nephew Joanne's cousin Michael's father
Hobbies	Needlework	Walking	Painting	Painting	Reading	Tennis
Age	58	29	5	62	86	34

Index

Game	Time (mins)	Communicative function/structure
Card games		
1 Indiscreet questions	45	ice breaker – asking questions
2 Snap	30	question tags
3 Swapping game	30	human qualities – negotiating
4 What is it?	30	describing things – passive
Agreeing and disagreeing games		
5 Likes and dislikes	20	expressing opinions
6 Things we have done	20	present perfect
7 Childhood memories	20	simple past: "used to" – "had to"
8 Feelings	20	adjectives and verbs that describe feelings
9 This and that	20	agreeing, disagreeing, and negotiating
10 Preposition merry-go-round	20	prepositions that are often confused
Information gap games		
11 People in our street 1	20	simple present
12 People in our street 2	20	describing people – defining relative clauses
13 Family photo	20	talking about relatives
Negotiating games		
14 My diary	30	making appointments – on/that
15 How well do you know each other?	30	"if" versus "when"
16 Doodles	20	expressing possibility – "could be"
17 Morning routine	30	simple present to express habitual action
18 What's the reason?	30	questions with "why"
19 Optimist and pessimist	20	"will"-future
20 Let's spend Saturday together	30	making suggestions: "we could" – "how about" – "we ought to"
Board games		
Snakes and ladders		
21 In a restaurant	45	complaining – polite questions
22 Could I ...?	30	polite requests – asking for permission
23 Spot the preposition	20	phrasal verbs
24 Fill the gaps	30	"for", "since", "ago" – simple past versus present perfect, simple and continuous